The NEW Intermittent Fasting Guide for Beginners

How to Lose Weight and Burn Fat Quickly

Contents

Quick snacks

Tomato Broccoli Soup

Fresh crab salad

Spinach salad with asparagus and strawberries

Spicy romaine lettuce with avocado & egg

Dessert

Chocolate brownies

Homemade strawberry ice cream with skyr

Sugar-free recipes

Fruity chia pudding

Black Forest cake

Stew with coconut and beans

Cauliflower casserole with ham

Christmas cookies without sugar

Delicious breakfast muffins

Refreshing lemonade

Oatmeal cup with yogurt & berries

Fruity popsicle

Bake sugar-free bread yourself

Homemade tomato ketchup

Couscous with tofu and spinach

Pizza with cauliflower batter

Tuna Egg Muffins

Sugar-free banana pancakes

hazelnut cake

Refreshing cherry and yogurt ice cream

Sugar-free lemon and orange iced tea

Sugar-free & healthy brownies

Sugar-free apple pie

Crispy chicken legs with red cabbage salad

Asian duck salad

Potato salad with apple and egg

Salad with potatoes tuna and egg

Sugar-free walnut raspberry muffins

Smoothies

Interval Fasting - How to Lose Weight and Burn Fat Quickly and Effectively with Intermittent Fasting

You have probably heard the term interval fasting before. Because this type of diet is particularly popular with celebrities and is therefore present in the media. The so-called interval fasting is a modern nutritional concept that is based on the diet of our ancestors. The special thing about interval fasting is that, compared to classic diets, it is not about what is eaten, but only about when food is consumed. Rules and prohibitions as well as hunger have no place in the diet. Interval fasting, therefore, means doing without - a concept that is enjoying increasing popularity and is also popular with celebrities.

Interval fasting is not a short-term diet, but a way of life. With it, it is very easy to lose weight while you sleep and to permanently reduce your weight. Everything you need to know about interval fasting can be found in this guide. In the following chapters, you will learn how interval fasting differs from classic therapeutic fasting and why it makes sense for almost everyone to eat according to this concept. We also give tips on practical implementation and point out the most common mistakes in interval fasting - so you can get started right away!

What is Interval Fasting?

To understand how you can lose weight with interval fasting, let us first explain the concept to you. The term describes a new type of fasting, in which mealtimes and fasting times alternate in a regular rhythm. In contrast to therapeutic fasting, interval fasting no longer means starving for days at a time, but only within certain time frames. Intermittent fasting is therefore also known as periodic or intermittent fasting. There are different variants in which the meal and fasting times are individually long. An interval can be spread over a day or a week.

The goal of this form of nutrition is to avoid eating for a few hours a day. During this time you are not allowed to eat and only unsweetened drinks are allowed. The rest of the day, however, can be eaten normally. However, normal food in this case does not mean that you do not have to pay attention to your diet during this time. If you overdo it with your calorie intake in this phase and do not stay in your calorie deficit, you will not be able to lose weight even with interval fasting. However, if you follow the basic rules of interval fasting, it's easy to shed pounds without starving.

The interval fasting goes back to our ancestors and was practically adopted by them. It can be assumed that before the constant availability of food through livestock and arable farming, people did not always have food and were therefore forced to fast. They were healthy and fit, had athletic bodies, and were not overweight - so periodic fasting seems effective and paying off. This basic idea has now been transferred to interval fasting. There are several different models for modern interval fasting, from which you can choose the right model according to your preferences or the daily routine. The most common model is the 16: 8 model, in which you fast for 16 hours and eat 8 hours a day. The 16: 8 method is also the variant preferred by celebrities because it can be easily integrated into everyday life. In our guide, we will also introduce you to the other options so that you get a comprehensive picture of interval fasting.

What is the idea behind the nutritional concept of interval fasting?

As already mentioned, the fasting interval is based on the diet of our ancestors before cattle and agriculture. Man is by nature prepared for the fact that he does not have the necessary food available at all times. But he survives this hunger well because the human body builds up energy reserves in the body for this case. These are stored in organs and tissues and can be used if necessary. Although today there are usually no more sudden famines and most people are well cared for, people have retained this mode of survival in the event of an emergency. This mode makes clever use of interval fasting through specific eating and fasting times. By fasting, i.e. the temporary withdrawal of food, the energy stores are opened and the metabolism works more effectively.

It is assumed that the regular and extensive fasting periods will bring the blood sugar level to a level and that the body will get the necessary energy from the fat reserves during the fasting phase. In this way, fat burning is effectively promoted and is much more active than if you eat all day. For example, those who consistently do not eat any food for 16 hours in the popular 16: 8 method and do without sugary drinks slip into fat burning. Studies have shown that you can lose weight much faster and better than people who eat food throughout the day. Researchers speak of a weight loss of up to 5 kilograms per week. But be careful: If you have even a small snack or a drink containing sugar during the fasting period, you will stop your fat burning immediately!

Effective interval fasting - this is how it works

The basic principle of interval fasting is very simple: You can eat normally at certain hours of the day, while no food and only sugar-free drinks are consumed in the remaining hours. During the eating phase, you can eat food without restrictions, although it is of course important to ensure that the food is balanced and healthy. Even with interval fasting, weight loss is only possible if you stay within your calorie deficit.

The most important thing is that you listen to your body. As soon as you notice that you are hungry and your stomach growls without a break, this is a sign from your body that it needs more energy and cannot cope with the waiver. Such a situation can occur especially in the initial phase because the body cannot adjust to the new diet so quickly and has to get used to it slowly. Since starvation is not supposed to be the purpose of interval fasting, it is recommended in such cases to follow the feeling and instead shorten the intervals accordingly. As a rule, you will no longer feel hungry after a few days, as the body quickly gets used to the new rhythm. Then you can slowly lengthen the intervals again.

In addition to proper nutrition, exercise is an elementary part of interval fasting. Sport or exercise are always part of the process if you want to burn fat effectively and permanently reduce your weight. Additional exercise in the morning is ideal for this purpose, as it boosts fat burning enormously on an empty stomach and can thus lead to even greater weight loss.

What models are there?

Depending on your preferences and your personal daily rhythm, you can choose from various models which intervals suit you best. Those who work a lot and have to do physically demanding activities may often forget to eat anyway but need the energy to be able to perform well. Other people find it particularly difficult not to be allowed to eat anything in the evening or at night. In these cases, you can either shift the rhythm accordingly or you have to find a method that can be reconciled with your everyday life. We would like to briefly introduce you to the different options:

The 16: 8 method

The 16: 8 method is the most popular and popular variant of interval fasting. This is also the rhythm most prominent nutritional advocates use for themselves. The main reason why the 16: 8 method is so popular is that it is the easiest to implement. Therefore, it is also well suited for beginners who want to discover interval fasting for themselves first. Since sleep is integrated into the 16 hours of fasting, you can use this method to lose weight while you sleep and do not have to prepare for a change.

With this variant, you are allowed to eat eight hours a day and then have to fast for 16 hours. In the fasting period, however, the daily sleep is already integrated, so that it is usually not very difficult to go without food. Due to the daily alternation between fasting and eating, there are hardly any restrictions in everyday life. After a short time, the changes in the rhythm are no longer noticeable. You simply skip breakfast or have dinner very early and then oversleep much of the fasting period. In any case, experts recommend integrating at least eight hours of sleep into the fasting interval to activate fat burning. Too little sleep inhibits this and would be counterproductive for successful weight loss.

In the 16: 8 method, everything is allowed during the eating phase. Of course, normal food does not mean that you can stuff yourself with fast food and still lose weight. The same applies here: the diet should be healthy and balanced. Extremely high-calorie intake is not the goal of interval fasting; instead, if you want to lose weight, there should be a calorie deficit at the end of the eating period. However, you do not have to do without complete meals in this model, as it is possible to eat early in the evening or have breakfast very late. All foods are strictly forbidden during the fasting period. In this phase, fat burning is to be activated, as the body, after consuming the available energy from carbohydrates, falls back on the fat reserves and begins to convert them. However, this can only work if you stick to the fasting period and do not eat anything during this time. Even a small snack or a sweetened drink will stop the burning of fat as it provides the body with energy from another source.

The only thing allowed during the fasting period is unsweetened drinks. It is recommended that you drink plenty of fluids such as tea or water or black coffee while you are fasting. As a rule, going without food shouldn't be a problem, as you will oversleep a large part of the fasting period anyway. However, since it is not healthy to avoid fluids, you should not forget to drink and consume at least two liters of water during the fasting period. Celebrities swear by the 16: 8 method because it promises enormous weight losses of up to five kilos per week if carried out consistently.

Our tip: Coffee is a real all-around talent. It perks you up and at the same time has an appetite-suppressing effect. This makes it well suited to appear energetic despite fasting and to survive the fasting period without any problems. However, you should only consume it unsweetened so as not to provide the body with an alternative source of energy. Also, drink the last cup before 5 p.m. to be able to fall asleep well in the evening.

The 36:12 method

The 36:12 method is a modified form of the 16: 8 method. In this variant, however, you are not allowed to eat anything for 36 hours and can then eat for 12 hours as required. Since the fasting interval with this variant is already very long, it is not suitable for everyone. Especially people with a stressful and demanding everyday life will quickly feel tired and emaciated from the long period without eating. For experienced riders, the 36:12 variant is certainly an option.

The 24:24 method

The 24:24 interval fasting model is particularly simple: You are not allowed to eat anything for 24 hours and can then eat whatever you want for 24 hours. This method has the advantage that it is easy to keep to the rhythm and that no calculations or planning are required. They just eat one day and not one. The intervals here are equally long and the fasting period is therefore easy to bear.

The 5: 2 method

After the 16: 8 method, the 5: 2 method is one of the most popular models of interval fasting. This is mainly because it is well suited for working people and that it is the only variant in which you can eat longer than you have to fast. The 5: 2 method allows you to eat normally five days a week and then not the other two days of the week. The two fasting days should, if possible, always fall on the same day of the week to create a regular rhythm and to be able to keep the phases.

There is another special feature of this method: On the fasting days you do not have to go completely without food, you just have to limit your calorie intake. This means that 500 calories per day are allowed for women and 600 calories for men. When and in what form these amounts are consumed is up to you and has no relevance for successful interval fasting. The calories ingested should come from lean protein, low-sugar fruits or vegetables. Carbohydrates in pasta, potatoes or bread should be avoided if possible. This also has the advantage for you that with a calorie intake of 500 or 600 calories you can eat a lot and feel full despite the fasting period. The 5: 2 method has the advantage that it works completely without feeling hungry and you as the user never have the feeling that you have to do without something or limit yourself.

The 5: 2 variant is ideal for everyone who has to work or study during the week and for whom another method of interval fasting is difficult to implement. The fasting days can then easily be carried out on the weekend or days off so that you can continue to be fully productive and concentrated at work or school. In addition, this model is just right for everyone who tends to give up and who has often experienced disappointments with other diets. Here you can eat what you want for five days and concentrate on the two days of fasting on looking forward to the upcoming eating phase. Since you don't even have to go completely without food on the fasting days, perseverance is even easier.

It is recommended not to use too much energy on fasting days in the 5: 2 method so as not to stress the body too much. On the two days during the fasting period, you should therefore avoid hard workouts and only do light exercises and movements. Long walks, pilates, swimming or yoga are ideal for fasting intervals. As in all variants of interval fasting, exercise is part of the concept, so you can plan your units on other days. The morning is best suited for sports units, as you will then be more productive due to the natural rhythm and additionally boost your metabolism.

It all depends on the right food - the diet for interval fasting

In general, you can eat at will during the meal phases. There is no calorie requirement to be adhered to. Nevertheless, every user should orientate himself on his calorie requirement and not exceed it if possible. With interval fasting, too, of course, weight loss is only possible with a calorie deficit. At the end of the day, there should be a deficit in your calorie balance if you want to lose weight over the long term. How high the personal need for calories depends on various factors. For example, age, height, weight, fitness, and other properties are decisive.

In principle, you can consume food within the scope of your personal calorie requirement. Of course, you should make sure that the foods you eat are as healthy as possible. The uncontrolled and massive consumption of sugary foods and fast food is not the point of interval fasting. The point here is to pay attention to your diet during the meal periods and to consume it consciously. Ingredients such as white flour, refined carbohydrates and sugar should be avoided if possible, as they can greatly increase blood sugar levels. In addition, animal fats from poultry, fish and meat are taboo. You should also avoid alcohol and soft drinks if you wanted to lose weight with interval fasting. Instead, when drinking, non-carbonated water is used. All the forbidden foods lead to food cravings and slow down fat burning. Instead, a diet with fillers like vegetables makes a lot more sense during the eating phases.

Still, starvation is not what interval fasting is supposed to be. If you feel extremely hungry, it is a sign that your body is not getting enough of the calories you have consumed. Listen to your gut instinct and if so, reduce the fasting periods accordingly. Food cravings that you feed with unhealthy food are counterproductive and should therefore be avoided whenever possible. Anyone who consciously and consistently carries out interval fasting will quickly notice that the body can cope very well with this form of nutrition. He adapts quickly and learns to work with the given rhythm. Interval fasting is also so popular because it not only brings success but can also do so without restrictions and starvation.

What successes does interval fasting promise?

We have already spoken several times of the enormous successes that interval fasting can bring with it. But what is it actually about? For people who want to reduce their weight effectively, the weight loss that interval fasting brings with it is certainly of particular interest. Studies show that with consistent interval fasting, the appropriate diet, and accompanying exercise, weight losses of up to five kilos per week are possible. These successes are of course enormous, also in comparison to other diets - and all without going hungry!

In addition to rapid weight loss, intermittent fasting has other positive effects on your life. The new nutritional rhythm effectively boosts fat burning and shows lasting success. With periodic fasting, you can find your desired weight in a short time and, in contrast to most diets, maintain it if you continue your diet accordingly. This means that the much-feared yo-yo effect, which occurs with almost all diets, does not occur and you can improve your well-being permanently.

In addition, interval fasting naturally also has health effects. With periodic fasting, you can prevent high blood pressure, which has a positive effect on your overall physical condition. In addition, the mood is lightened by the new nutritional rhythm, because you eat a healthy and balanced diet and the body is not busy breaking down harmful ingredients. Regular fasting has been shown to prevent many other diseases.

That is why there is no yo-yo effect with interval fasting

The problem with many diets is that although weight is lost, it is immediately gained again as soon as the diet returns to normal. On the one hand, this happens because the diets usually involve radical changes in diet or calorie reductions. After the end of the diet, the body takes back what was withheld from it during the diet. On the other hand, the body mainly loses water on short-term diets. However, fat, which would have to be broken down for permanent weight loss, is not reduced. The water is stored again immediately as soon as the diet has ended. In many cases, the yo-yo effect brings even more weight with it after the diet than was previously lost. At the same time, this also means that most diets are associated with an enormous potential for frustration and have no effect in the long term or are even counterproductive.

It is different from interval fasting: Periodic fasting is not a diet in the classic sense, as the body does not have to do without certain foods or ingredients. Nor is there any extreme reduction in calories associated with the change in diet. Interval fasting is not about what is eaten, but when. Since interval fasting is a way of life that is implemented holistically and carried out permanently, no yo-yo effect can occur. The diet is changed not just for a certain time, but forever. In addition, intermittent fasting not only breaks down water from the body but also effectively boosts fat burning, which is of course much more effective for serious weight loss. By breaking down fat, weight is permanently reduced and health and fitness are significantly improved.

Who is interval fasting for?

If you are now fundamentally convinced of interval fasting, you may be wondering whether this type of diet is also an option for you. Basically, interval fasting is suitable for everyone who wants to decide on a healthy way of life and is ready to consistently and consciously bring a new rhythm into their life. The only requirement is the will to change one's life permanently with the help of a new eating rhythm and to find a new sense of well-being, fitness and the desired weight.

All adult people who do not have any health problems can implement the interval fast without great difficulty and adjust their diet accordingly. This does not require a lot of preparation. Since the diet itself does not have to be changed, you do not have to get used to it if you are already eating a healthy and balanced diet. The only change is the intervals that dictate when you are allowed to eat and when not. So you don't have to buy any specific groceries, do not go without anything or cook according to given recipes. If you decide to live according to the principle of interval fasting, you can start at any time!

Intermittent fasting is particularly suitable for people who already do not like breakfast or do not eat anything in the evening. There can be various reasons for not eating one of the meals. Whether it happens out of personal preference or due to a lack of time is initially irrelevant. However, skipping a meal, as usual, is a good prerequisite for interval fasting, as such people do not have to get used to a new rhythm at all. The existing behavior can then be optimally adopted, especially in the 16: 8 rhythm, since breakfast or dinner is usually not served here either.

In addition, interval fasting is exactly the right thing for people who do not want to be restricted by rules and prohibitions and who may have already failed other diets for these reasons. In almost all diets you have to actively do without something - be it a certain food, carbohydrates, fats or something else. This is not the case with periodic fasting. Rather, it is a nutritional concept that permanently changes eating behavior. Apart from the time adjustment to the intervals, there are no further requirements, so that you do not have to comply with any rules or prohibitions. This makes interval fasting more fun than other diets, and users don't feel restricted or patronized. The usual defiance or protest reactions do not occur so that motivating successes can be seen quickly.

For people who, due to their stressful and hectic everyday life, often forget to eat during the day, interval fasting comes at the right time. You can take this opportunity and integrate it into your new form of nutrition. In this way, the fasting periods can be survived virtually unnoticed. Thanks to the large selection of different methods, everyone will find the right concept for interval fasting to integrate into their everyday life.

There is one factor that should not be underestimated when it comes to interval fasting: As a result of the few and regular meals, there is usually much less work. You no longer have to cook, smear bread or prepare fruit and vegetables as often. This not only saves you time but also means fewer dirty dishes. Because of the inevitably restricted meals, interval fasting is the ideal method for people who tend to be lazy or who have little time to take care of the household.

Of course, there are also numerous people who don't want to do things by halves. This means that these people do not like to be restricted and either completely or not at all. Interval fasting is also the optimal solution for this group of people. During the fasting intervals, they completely and consistently forego food, while they do not have to accept any restrictions at all during the eating phases. Such people are often people who have tried many diets and nutritional concepts for themselves but have not achieved any success with any of them. Frustration and anger are not good prerequisites for losing weight successfully. Instead, interval fasting can be a good alternative.

As a final and important factor, we would like to bring the social aspect into play. Many diets and forms of nutrition can not only be combined not only with your own but, above all, with everyday social life. Those who want to continue to participate in social life often find themselves in a conflict when trying to lose weight. The peer pressure is often so great that when going out with friends or at club meetings you throw all good resolutions overboard and treat yourself to something delicious or a cold beer. Interval fasting is ideal for people who want to continue to participate in social life and are very involved here. Restrictions or a guilty conscience are a thing of the past. For example, you can still go out to eat with friends without restricting yourself. It is only important that you adhere to the intervals. This is easily possible by planning the meeting with your best friend accordingly or by scheduling the visit to grandma at the right time. For people with a lot of social obligations, interval fasting is a good way to balance private life and diet.

Who is interval fasting not suitable for?

Even if interval fasting promises great success, not everyone can achieve success with this nutritional concept. There are even groups for whom this type of diet can be rather unhealthy. This includes children and toddlers, pregnant women, people with chronic conditions such as diabetes or thyroid disease, the elderly, and people with an eating disorder.

Even people who have to operate heavy machines at work and therefore need a lot of energy and full attention should rather avoid interval fasting. Fasting can lead to concentration problems or symptoms of fatigue. However, the 5: 2 method, which allows fasting on non-working days, can be considered for such people. For people who work in shifts and therefore do not have a fixed daily routine and sleep rhythm, it is as good as impossible to adhere to the intervals.

Likewise, the concept of nutrition is not for people who take medication or drink alcohol. This is mainly because the effects of alcohol on an empty stomach are increased. Of course, you shouldn't consume more alcohol than you can handle. However, the reduced food intake can lead to increased effects that cannot be taken into account. The same applies to pharmaceutical substances on an empty stomach. This can lead to side effects when used in combination with interval fasting.

If you are not ready to change your diet permanently, you have come to the wrong address with interval fasting. This concept requires discipline and consistency to be effective over the long term. There are no major restrictions or changes when it comes to what can be eaten but you have to stick to the interval phases. If you do not do this you will not boost your metabolism sufficiently and will not switch to fat burning. Even if the success of interval fasting in the form of weight loss is quick, the nutritional concept is not for people who just want to lose a few pounds quickly.

This is what a day with the 16: 8 method could look like

If you choose the 16: 8 interval fasting method, the day starts quite early. In the morning, around seven o'clock, the alarm clock should ring. You are now at your top performance and should therefore start with an exercise session. It is best to drink one or two glasses of water before exercising. Exercising in the morning can stimulate your metabolism and burn extra calories to help you stay in calorie deficit throughout the day.

After you've showered and freshened up, the day begins. You either drive to work, go to the office or work from home. Maybe the housework is waiting for you or you can take care of the children. Treat yourself to a cup of tea or coffee beforehand to start the day full of energy and motivation. Take a break from time to time during work, drink coffee and plenty of water.

Lunch should take place around 1 p.m. It is the first meal of the day so you will enjoy it to the full. Lunch should be a balanced meal of protein, vegetables and meat or fish. Whole grain rice and whole wheat pasta are also allowed. After your meal, you can have an espresso to keep you awake for hours to come.

You should drink the last cup of coffee of the day by 5 p.m. at the latest. Because coffee contains caffeine, it wakes you up and prevents you from falling asleep. They find it difficult to fall asleep and cannot reach the restful and necessary deep sleep phase. This is why you should avoid caffeine after 5 p.m. if you want to lead a healthy life.

In the evening you can do another exercise if necessary. The muscles are now warmed up from the day, so strength exercises are particularly suitable for the evening hours. By exercising, you can sleep well in the evening and have the good feeling of having achieved something.

The eating phase is over around 8 p.m. Dinner should now be eaten. Eat proteins, vegetables, and good carbohydrates again. At the end of the eating phase, a dessert is now also allowed. This can consist of fruit or quark. It lies lightly in the stomach and does not burden digestion too much overnight. If you enjoy having a beer or a glass of wine every now and then, you can do so with dinner as well. Anyone who drinks alcoholic beverages later in the evening not only risks unhealthy sleep, but also disturbs the fasting period - because as soon as a sugary drink is drunk, fat burning is interrupted during the fasting interval or, accordingly, cannot even begin.

You should go to sleep around 10pm or 11pm. It is believed that eight hours of sleep are necessary for a functioning metabolism and a healthy lifestyle. Give your body the necessary rest so that it can relax and regenerate. Sleep also has the advantage that the fasting period passes unnoticed by you and you can literally become slim while you sleep.

With the 16: 8 method, a new day begins in the morning at the same rhythm. Each day should be roughly the same in structure so that the body can quickly get used to the new rhythm. It doesn't matter whether you skip breakfast or dinner. It is only important that the intervals are adhered to. You can decide for yourself which meal you want to skip and which you cannot do without. It is also possible to keep all meals and reduce the time between them. You can have breakfast at 10 a.m., have lunch at 1 p.m. and prepare dinner around 6 p.m. - this process would also be possible within the meal interval.

Interval fasting against hyperacidity

We've already told you that interval fasting has numerous health benefits. Fasting allows the body to regenerate and detoxify. At the beginning of the fasting period, side effects such as headaches can occur, as metabolic residues are transported out of the body. To aid this process, drinking during the fasting interval is essential. A quantity of at least two liters of water a day is recommended.

Since many people become acidic through the consumption of sweets and sugary foods, meat and alcohol, it is important that the acid-base balance is rebalanced at regular intervals. You can restore this balance with interval fasting. Intermittent fasting has long been an effective aid not only for people who are overweight, but can also help with hyperacidity.

You can easily tell that you suffer from hyperacidity from various symptoms. It manifests itself in fatigue, sleep disorders, exhaustion, digestive problems, migraine attacks and headaches. Brittle hair and nails can also be an indication that acidification is present.

Certain foods that can be cleverly incorporated into the menu during interval fasting can help against acidification. These are so-called base formers such as potatoes, fresh herbs, spinach, potatoes, lupine, sprouts and spices such as chili or ginger. You can also incorporate these base builders into your diet outside of the interval to prevent over-acidification.

The numerous benefits of interval fasting

So far we have not found any negative aspects of interval fasting. It can be easily integrated into everyday life, has no restrictions and has positive effects on your health. Interval fasting results in numerous advantages for you in your everyday life. In addition to losing weight, which has a positive overall effect on health, the nutritional concept also has other effects. Targeted fasting can slightly lower blood pressure and thus prevent high blood pressure. In addition, the balanced energy supply brightens the mood - you feel fit, motivated, healthy and lively!

The regular fasting periods balance the cholesterol and blood sugar levels. Fasting, therefore, reduces the risk of diabetes. In addition, the intestinal flora is improved by interval fasting, so that stomach and intestinal complaints occur less frequently. People with sensitive stomachs can see significant improvements from intermittent fasting. There is also scientific evidence that fasting can have a positive effect on rheumatic diseases.

During Lent, the cells have enough time to regenerate, which is generally healthy for the body. Interval fasting is also healthy for your brain. Studies have shown that you can effectively counteract dementia with this method.

Another advantage is that there are no prohibitions associated with interval fasting. This not only means that the nutritional concept is easy to implement for everyone, but also that you can live without restrictions and rules and can easily integrate interval fasting into your everyday life. Since it is not a diet, but a holistic nutritional concept that affects the entire life, there is no yo-yo effect with interval fasting.

Interval Fasting For Beginners: Some Tips for Beginners

- ·Always listen to your body! He knows what's good for him. If you suffer from extreme hunger or spontaneous food cravings, it shows you that the fasting intervals are too long. Changing your diet too suddenly is not good and can overwhelm the body. In this case, you should adjust the phases accordingly and only slowly extend them again until the desired rhythm is achieved.

- Take enough fluids! We recommend at least two to three liters of water a day. Unsweetened tea and black coffee are also allowed during the fasting phase. However, milk and sugar are taboo as they would stop fat metabolism. Sufficient fluids are important to prevent tiredness and headaches and to stimulate metabolism.

- Don't set yourself too high a goal! The body cannot cope with too extreme a change in lifestyle. Therefore, it is better to slowly increase the intervals. We recommend starting with a 12-hour fasting phase. Everyone should be able to cope with this, especially if one assumes that daily sleep is already integrated into this phase.

- Move! On the one hand, you can burn calories through exercise. On the other hand, stress is one of the main reasons for food cravings and should therefore be avoided if possible. Of course, this is not always possible. Exercise is an alternative way to reduce stress and distract yourself. Exercise is therefore a good way to get used to the new rhythm, especially at the beginning of interval fasting.

- Find yourself a distraction! Many people don't eat out of hunger, but out of boredom. Distraction is therefore the best way to prevent unnecessary eating. If you don't have time to think about food, you won't either. If you fill the day well with work, friends, hobbies, and exercise, you will find it easy to get through the fasting intervals.

- Keep going! Interval fasting isn't just a short diet that lets you shed a few pounds quickly. Instead, intermittent fasting is more of an attitude towards life that you have to fit into on a long-term basis. By permanently changing your eating habits, you can achieve long-term success.

- Don't let setbacks discourage you! Even if you sometimes believe that you will not be able to keep up the intermittent fasting or that you do not keep the intervals, it does not have to be the end. It is important to understand the reasons and work on them. If the fasting intervals are too long for you and you are hungry, you should adjust the phases individually.

- Look for the support! Losing weight on its own isn't that much fun anyway. So it makes sense when looking for a fasting partner. You can talk to like-minded people about nutrition and also eat, cook or do sports together. In addition, you don't feel alone if things don't go the way you want them to. You can share successes and difficulties with a fasting partner.

Common mistakes to avoid

Interval fasting is a fairly simple nutritional concept. Apart from the intervals, the user does not have to adhere to any rules, prohibitions or regulations. You can't go wrong there - you should think. But users are always disappointed because they do not achieve the promised success. And of course, there is a reason for that. Therefore, we would like to introduce you to the most common mistakes in interval fasting that you should avoid if you want to achieve lasting success:

Mistake 1: Set too high demands on yourself and the nutritional concept

Many people believe that with interval fasting you can change your diet and then achieve immediate results. But it's not that simple. It may be that the body is overwhelmed with the sudden change in diet, which can be expressed in hunger and malaise. That's why it makes a lot more sense to set small goals and slowly increase them. In most cases, it is recommended to start with a fasting interval of 12 hours. This is then increased slowly and evenly according to the chosen method.

Mistake 2: The fasting variant does not fit the life model

Some users do not manage to permanently integrate interval fasting into their everyday life. But this is mainly since you have not selected the right method for yourself. The interval fasting should fit the life model: For example, some people do not like breakfast and can therefore easily do without it, while others have no energy to cope with their stressful everyday life without the morning meal. It is also quite possible that interval fasting cannot be reconciled with a life model at all - then you should understand this and resort to a different nutritional concept.

Mistake 3: Aside from the intervals, nothing matters

The assumption that no factors other than observing the intervals play a role in interval fasting is wrong. Even if you keep the fasting period strictly, you will gain weight if you stuff yourself with unhealthy fast food during the eating phase. The energy balance should not be neglected in any nutritional concept. The same applies to intermittent fasting: only those who have a negative energy balance will lose weight in the long term. This means that the calorie consumption must be greater than the calorie intake. Large amounts of calories can often be offset by an additional exercise session. It also helps to chew meals thoroughly to develop food awareness and a feeling of satiety. The diet should always be balanced and enjoyed. But be careful: Too little food is also bad, as the metabolism slows down in this case to save energy and stock up on supplies. Instead of energy, which is not available, muscle mass is then reduced. However, this is urgently needed for energy consumption. Strength training offers an opportunity to break out of this vicious circle.

Mistake 4: Insufficient fluid intake

In addition to nutrition, drinking is also very important. During the fasting period, the only thing you can consume is fluids. Water and unsweetened tea and black coffee are allowed. The drinks help burn fat and a daily amount of around two to three liters of water is recommended. Fluid intake also reduces the feeling of hunger, so it will help you get through the fasting periods without cravings. It also prevents headaches and fatigue.

Interval fasting vs. therapeutic fasting - what's the difference?

After reading our guide, you may be wondering how interval fasting differs from therapeutic fasting. The classic therapeutic fasting according to Dr. Otto Buchinger has been around since the 1930s. In this fasting method, solid food is completely avoided for a certain period of up to three weeks. Juices, tea and broth may be partially consumed, otherwise, only water is allowed. Even if the calorie intake during therapeutic fasting is extremely low, weight reduction is not the aim of this method. It is more about stimulating the metabolism and detoxifying the body. Many people take a therapeutic fast once or twice a year to do something good for their bodies. However, the concept is not suitable for people who have previous illnesses such as diabetes and cannot be easily integrated into everyday life, as its use is associated with a lot of hunger, fatigue, difficulty concentrating, and mood swings.

While therapeutic fasting is only a temporary application, interval fasting is more of a holistic way of life. This means that the diet is changed according to the concept and this method is retained permanently for the future. In doing so, you make use of the positive effects of fasting on the metabolism and can use them if necessary to burn fat in a targeted manner. Those who permanently integrate interval fasting into their everyday life can easily maintain their weight. As a rule, there is no yo-yo effect, as occurs with other diets or after therapeutic fasting. In addition, you do not have to pay attention to anything besides the interval phases when interval fasting. Even with this concept, the diet should be designed to be healthy and balanced, but there are no restrictions or prohibitions. That is why intermittent fasting does not involve starving - on the contrary: if the body cannot cope with the given intervals, you should listen to your feelings and adjust the phases accordingly.

Conclusion: Interval fasting is the renunciation of the renunciation!

Now that you have read our guide intensively, you will quickly find out whether interval fasting is a suitable nutritional method for you. Overall, it can be said that intermittent fasting is not a classic diet, but a holistic diet that affects your entire life.

Interval fasting is quite simple: you are allowed to eat at certain times of the day, not at other times. The intervals depend on the selected method and contain different numbers of hours. Nothing is to be eaten during the fasting period, only unsweetened drinks are allowed. In return, you can eat whatever you want during the eating phase.

There are no restrictions on the interval fasting lifestyle. The only factor to consider is adherence to fasting and eating intervals. If you stick to the given times, you will soon see results. There are no restrictions, bans or rules on what can be eaten. Of course, the diet should remain healthy and balanced, and there must be a calorie deficit to lose weight. Extreme calorie intake during the eating phases is not the goal of interval fasting, and starvation is also not necessary. So it is possible to lose weight with interval fasting without starving and having no noticeable restrictions.

But interval fasting can not only reduce your weight. Those who permanently eat according to the nutritional concept will feel positive effects on the body and mind. Fasting is healthy and can prevent disease. Unless it is only carried out over a certain period, as is the case with therapeutic fasting, there is also no yo-yo effect.

In contrast to therapeutic fasting, interval fasting avoids cravings. It is therefore much easier to adhere to the change in diet and to get used to the fasting period over the long term. Interval fasting is not perceived as a restriction and therefore does not cause users to be in a bad mood. Through the targeted intake of beverages such as unsweetened tea or water as well as black coffee, the feeling of hunger can be specifically suppressed during the fasting phase.

Since there are many different models for interval fasting, the right variant should also be available for you. The various models can usually be easily integrated into the everyday life of the user. If you have to work during the week and need sufficient energy, you can, for example, use the 5: 2 method and drastically reduce your calorie intake on the weekend. Other people get along better with the variants in which fasting and eating phases are repeated in daily rhythms.

The 16: 8 method, which fasts for 16 hours a day and eight hours of eating is allowed, is particularly popular. Many celebrities swear by this variant of interval fasting, which is why the nutritional concept is particularly topical in the media. The model does not have any restrictions on nutrition and changes the daily routine only very slightly. The 16: 8 method can be easily integrated into the daily routine, as the sleep phase is added to the 16 hours and the fasting period can thus be easily overcome. So if you sleep eight hours a day, you only have to go without food in the four hours before and after - that shouldn't be a problem as a rule!

One thing should not be underestimated: All social obligations can still be fulfilled during the interval fasting, which would not be a matter of course for a diet. If you practice intermittent fasting, you can eat normally and only have to stick to certain times. For example, if you know you are going out to dinner with friends, you can do so without hesitation. You just have to go without breakfast to keep your rhythm.

Overall, it can be said that interval fasting means renouncing the renunciation. Unlike other diets, there are no rules or prohibitions, so you don't feel restricted and can continue to eat and enjoy what you love. Hunger shouldn't play a role in interval fasting - this is how weight loss is fun!

100 delicious recipes

Breakfast

Delicious Sunday rolls

4 servings

Preparation 5 minutes

Preparation 40-50 minutes

210 g ground and blanched almonds

½ packet of baking powder

4 egg whites

1 teaspoon salt

200 ml of hot water

35 g of ground psyllium husks

1. Preheat the oven to 175 ° C fan oven while you prepare the dough. So you can bake the rolls as soon as the dough is ready.

2. Mix all dry ingredients thoroughly in a bowl, then add the egg whites. The egg white does not have to be whipped, but can simply be added.

3. Mix all ingredients well, gradually adding the hot water. Make sure that the water is really extremely hot to make a perfect batter. The dough gradually reaches its correct consistency.

4. Divide the dough into four equal parts and form rolls from them. Place these on a baking sheet lined with baking paper and slide them into the preheated oven.

5. The rolls have to bake at 175 ° C for about 40 - 50 minutes until they have reached the desired degree of browning. Good Appetite!

Turkish menemen (scrambled eggs)

4 servings

Preparation 15 minutes

Preparation in 20 minutes

6 eggs

salt

20 g butter

1 dash of milk 3.5%

400 g cherry tomatoes

200 g green pointed peppers

1 small onion

10 ml of olive oil

1 hand of parsley

1. Put the eggs in a bowl, stir, add a dash of milk and season with salt.

2. Halve the cherry tomatoes, dice the pointed peppers and onions and fry them in the olive oil.

3. Put some butter in a pan and let it melt. (The pan must not get too hot!) Add the beaten egg and use a rubber scraper to scrape the scrambled eggs from the bottom of the pan whenever they start to stagnate. (Make sure that the scrambled eggs do not set too dry as they will still drag until serving!)

4. Put the finished scrambled eggs on a plate and roughly chop the parsley.

5. Now heat the olive oil in a pan and sweat the onions, bell peppers and tomatoes and season everything with salt and pepper.

6. Now put everything on the scrambled eggs. And sprinkle the scrambled eggs with fresh parsley.

Tip: tastes great with the above-mentioned Sunday bread rolls!

Breakfast bags with eggs and bacon

2 servings

Preparation 15 minutes

Preparation in 20 minutes

120 g mozzarella

3 eggs

40 g butter

4 slices of bacon

30 g almond flour

1. Melt the mozzarella in the microwave or a small saucepan. Please note that the cheese must not boil or fry! Meanwhile, preheat the oven to 200 ° C top / bottom heat.

2. Mix the almond flour with the liquid cheese to form a batter. Knead it thoroughly with your hands while it is still warm.

3. Divide the dough into two equal parts and roll the pieces out thinly with a rolling pin. Line the pieces of dough with two slices of bacon each. You can use this raw or, if necessary, fry it until crispy beforehand.

4. Melt the butter in a pan and prepare scrambled eggs from the eggs and season to taste with salt and pepper. The finished scrambled eggs are spread over the two pieces of dough.

5. Fold the dough pieces together so that they are closed on all sides and place them on the baking paper with the seam down. Pierce the pockets on the top to prevent them from popping.

6. Bake the breakfast bags at 200 ° C for about 15-20 minutes until they are adequately tanned and serve when they are fresh and hot.

Tip: You can fill the dough made from mozzarella and almond flour in any other way, for example with vegetables or meat. Enjoy your meal!

Low-carb protein pancakes

2 servings

Preparation 5 minutes

Preparation time 15 minutes

2 eggs

40 g butter

30 g of vanilla protein powder

1 banana

5 tbsp ground almonds or almond flour

1-2 tbsp xucker

Pinch of cinnamon

1. Whisk the eggs in a bowl and mash the banana with a fork.

2. Add protein powder, xucker, almonds or almond flour and mix briefly with the hand blender.

3. Add cinnamon to taste.

4. Heat the butter in a pan and add some batter with a medium ladle. **(The first time you might want to bake a small sample pancake, add a little more almonds or almond flour if necessary. Everyone likes it a little different.)**

5. Bake the pancakes until golden on both sides.

6. Serve

Tip: Tastes best with fruit skyr

Fruity Skyr

2 servings

Preparation 5 minutes

Preparation 10 minutes

250 grams of skyr

100 g frozen fruits (strawberries, cherries, blueberries, forest fruits) **(unsweetened !!)**

10 drops of stevia **(if necessary)**

Vanilla pulp from half a pod

1. Defrost the fruits in a glass bowl using the microwave and then cut them into small pieces with a knife.

2. Add stevia, vanilla and skyr and stir.

3. Possibly season with a little cinnamon if you use cherries.

green smoothie

1 serving

Preparation 5 minutes

Preparation 5 minutes

1 ½ apples

2/3 banana

10 baby spinach leaves

1/4 g pear

1 leaf of kale

1 slice of Inger

Knife point of Matcha

1. Peel all fruits and cut into pieces

2. Puree everything in the blender.

3. Serve fresh and with ice cubes!

Main courses

Juicy pizza with a tuna base

4 servings

Preparation 20 minutes

Preparation in 20 minutes

100 g chicory

30 g onions

50 g bacon

30 g paprika

1 egg

150 g canned tuna in oil

30 grams of cheddar

some butter

1. Preheat the oven to around 200 ° C. Drain the tuna thoroughly and mix with the egg to form a smooth batter.

2. Cut the vegetables, onions and bacon into small pieces and fry everything in a pan for about 5 minutes.

3. Spread the tuna mixture on a baking sheet and pour the mixture of bacon and vegetables evenly on top. Sprinkle the cheese on top and put everything in the oven for about 20 minutes.

Delicious salad with avocado & tuna

2 servings

Preparation 10 minutes

Preparation 10 minutes

2 eggs

2 tbsp balsamic vinegar

10 g onions

160 g avocado

90 g red oak leaf lettuce

6 olives

1 ½ tbsp olive oil

90 g tuna in water in the can

1. Boil the eggs firmly for about 10-15 minutes. Meanwhile, tear and wash the lettuce and place in a large bowl.

2. Cut the avocado into small cubes and add them to the bowl. Chop the onions and olives and add both.

3. Drain the tuna thoroughly and use a fork to cut it into small pieces that are also added to the salad.

4. After cooling, the eggs are also cut into small pieces and added to the salad. Drizzle with oil and balsamic vinegar and mix well before serving.

Soup with curry and prawns

2 servings

Preparation 20 minutes

Preparation in 20 minutes

salt and pepper

50 g cream

100 g coconut milk

2 teaspoons of curry powder

½ lime

3 tbsp coconut oil

400 ml vegetable stock

2 stalks of celery

½ stick of leek

½ red pepper

1 carrot

8 frozen king prawns

1. In preparation, first thaw the king prawns according to the package instructions and then wash them thoroughly with cold water. Place four of the prawns on a kebab skewer.

2. Peel the carrot and remove the seeds from the pepper. Thoroughly clean the leek and celery, then cut all the vegetables into small cubes.

3. Briefly sweat the diced vegetables with 1 tablespoon of coconut oil in a pan and pour the vegetable stock on top. Bring everything to a boil over high heat and finally add the curry powder. Now let the soup simmer for about 10 minutes over medium heat.

4. Wash the lime and rub the peel off. Add the zest and juice to the soup along with the coconut milk and cream. The soup should now only be kept warm and seasoned with salt and pepper.

5. Season the prawns with salt and pepper and fry them in the remaining coconut oil for about 1 minute on each side. Serve one skewer at a time with the soup.

Tasty feta souvlaki skewers

2 servings

Preparation 1 hour

Preparation time 15 minutes

100 g feta

½ red onion

1 clove of garlic

1 teaspoon dried thyme

salt and pepper

olive oil

½ lemon

3 stalks of parsley

½ teaspoon dried rosemary

1 teaspoon dried oregano

2 yellow peppers

150 g pork neck

1. Cut the feta into approx. 2 cm cubes. Chop the onions, garlic, chili and put everything in a bowl with 3 teaspoons of olive oil, thyme and a little salt. Put everything in the refrigerator until it goes on.

2. Squeeze out 1 tablespoon of lemon juice and mix it with finely chopped parsley, 1 tablespoon of olive oil, rosemary and oregano. Season generously with salt and pepper. Cut the meat into cubes about 3 cm and coat it with the marinade on all sides. Chill everything for at least 1 hour or overnight.

3. Cut the peppers into cubes and stick them alternately with the meat on kebab skewers. With the remaining olive oil, sear the souvlaki skewers over medium heat for about 2-3 minutes on each side.

4. Arrange the skewers with the feta in the marinade on two plates and enjoy a delicious Greek dish, keto-style!

Low-carb pasta with Bolognese

3-4 servings

Preparation 20 minutes

Preparation in 25 minutes

Salt, pepper, oregano, paprika powder

500 grams of minced meat

1 can of chopped tomatoes

1 onion

2 cloves of garlic

2 tbsp olive oil

2 tbsp tomato paste

400 ml vegetable stock

3-4 large zucchini

4 large carrots

1 handful of basil

1. Wash and peel the carrots and zucchini. After the peel has been removed, continue peeling until all of the zucchini and carrots have been completely peeled in ribbon noodle-like strips.

2. Now put some olive oil in a pan and steam the carrots and zucchini strips until they are cooked through.

3. Cut the peeled onions and garlic into fine cubes. Now fry the minced beef in a pan in olive oil, add the onion and garlic and sauté everything. Make sure the pan is hot so that the meat roasts and does not boil. This gives flavor! Now add the tomato paste and roast this again and remove everything with the broth.

4. Add the chopped tomatoes and season the Bolognese with salt, pepper, oregano and paprika powder.

5. Now add the already steamed zucchini and vegetable strips and toss the "pasta" again. Serve the pasta with fresh basil.

Fillet of beef with Caesar salad

2 servings

Preparation 20 minutes

Preparation in 25 minutes

250 g, beef fillet (1.5 cm thick)

salt and pepper

2 teaspoons of rapeseed oil

400 g small lettuce hearts

4 tbsp vegetable broth

Chili flakes

100 g of cocktail tomatoes

80 g natural yogurt (0.1% fat)

2 teaspoons of white wine vinegar

20 g grated parmesan cheese

20 g capers

2 teaspoons of chives rolls

1. Preheat the oven to 100 degrees. Slide the oven grid with a fat tray underneath onto the middle rail. Salt and pepper the fillets and fry them in the oil in a pan on both sides. Remove, dab and let simmer on the rack in the oven for 15 to 20 minutes.

2. Clean the lettuce hearts, wash, pat dry and quarter lengthways. Fry in the still hot pan over low heat for 2 minutes. Add the stock and cook for another 2 minutes. Season with salt, pepper and chili flakes. Wash and halve the tomatoes.

3. Mix the yoghurt, vinegar and parmesan, season with salt and pepper. Thinly slice the beef fillet and arrange on a plate with the lettuce hearts and tomatoes. Pour dressing over it and sprinkle everything with capers and chives.

Pikeperch fillet on zucchini and mango vegetables

2 servings

Preparation 20 minutes

Preparation in 25 minutes

150 g pikeperch fillet (or other firm white fish fillet)

2 teaspoons of lemon juice

sea-salt

1 medium-sized zucchini (approx. 250 g)

2 tbsp olive oil

1 teaspoon chopped ginger

2 tbsp soy sauce

0.5 mango

black pepper from the mill

2.5 stalks of Thai basil

1. Rinse and dab the fish, drizzle with lemon juice and season with salt. Wash the zucchini, cut off the ends. Cut the vegetables in half slices. Heat the olive oil in a large saucepan and fry the ginger and zucchini in it. Continue frying, stirring, until the zucchini is lightly browned.

2. Deglaze with soy sauce and enough water to cover the bottom of the pot with liquid. Put the fish on top of the vegetables. Close the lid and let the fish steam for 5 minutes.

3. Cut the mango into strips. Wash the Thai basil, remove the leaves. Put the mango and basil on top of the fish. Grind the pepper over it and cook for another 2 minutes with the lid closed.

Chili with eggplant (vegetarian)

2 servings

Preparation 20 minutes

Preparation in 25 minutes

100 g soy strips (fine)

Vegetable broth for soaking

2 large carrots

1 large vegetable onion

3 cloves of garlic

1 bell pepper

2 tbsp olive oil (plus olive oil for drizzling)

2 teaspoons of harissa

2 tbsp curry

2 tbsp tomato paste

1 small can of kidney beans

1 eggplant

salt

1 large can of tomatoes

Juice of half a lemon

1. Soak the soy shredded meat in the stock according to the instructions on the package. Peel the carrots, onion and garlic and cut into cubes. Clean the peppers and cut into cubes.

2. Heat the oil in a large ovenproof roasting pan, add the harissa, curry and tomato paste and fry with the oil. Add the vegetables and fry them. Then add soy schnitzel with broth and continue to fry while stirring until the liquid has evaporated. Preheat the oven to 200 degrees.

3. Drain the kidney beans, rinse and place in the roaster. Wash the eggplant and cut into thick slices. Slice the canned tomatoes in the tin, place half in the roasting pan. Cover the vegetable mixture with eggplant slices. Salt and sprinkle with curry. Drizzle with lemon juice and olive oil. Cover with the rest of the canned tomatoes.

4. Add enough water to cover the bottom of the mold. Cook in the oven at 200 degrees for 45–50 minutes. The eggplant slices should be tender and

cooked through. Delicious with: corn tortilla chips and avocado.

Vegetable Lasagna

4 servings

Preparation 20 minutes

Preparation in 25 minutes

200 g tomatoes

100 g yellow hot peppers

100 g red hot peppers

100 g carrots

100 g celeriac

2 tbsp olive oil

300 g ground beef

1 teaspoon curry powder

Sea salt, black pepper

150 ml vegetable stock

100 ml coconut milk

1 teaspoon honey

2 eggplants

1. Preheat the oven to 160 degrees.

2. Wash tomatoes and peppers, cut in half and dice. Peel and dice the carrots and celeriac. Put everything aside in a bowl.

3. Heat the olive oil in a pan, fry the minced meat for 5 minutes. Season with curry, salt and pepper. Add the vegetables and fry them briefly. Add vegetable stock and simmer for 15 minutes. Season the meat and vegetable ragout with coconut milk and honey.

4. Wash the eggplant and cut into thin slices.

5. Layer the minced meat and vegetable ragout alternately with eggplant slices in a baking dish, top with a layer of vegetables. Bake in the oven for 35 minutes.

Exotic chicken skewers

2 servings

Preparation 20 minutes

Preparation in 25 minutes

1 clove of garlic

0.5 lemons

2 tbsp olive oil

0.3 tsp curry

0.3 tsp red paprika powder

1 teaspoon sesame seeds

Sea salt, pepper

250 g pineapple

250 g red pepper

300 g chicken breast

4 wooden skewers

1. Peel the garlic and chop very finely. Squeeze the lemon. Mix both with olive oil, curry, paprika powder, sesame, salt and pepper to a marinade.

2. Peel and core the pineapple and bell pepper. Clean the chicken breast. Cut both with the bell pepper into pieces about 2 x 2 cm in size.

3. Put the meat, pineapple and paprika alternately on the skewers. Spread the marinade over it and let it steep in the refrigerator for about half an hour.

4. Wash the eggplant and cut into thin slices.

5. Fry the skewers and eggplant on the grill or in a grill pan.

Quiche with blueberries and goat cheese

6 servings

Preparation 20 minutes

Preparation time 45 minutes

1 piece of spring onion

200 g blueberries

100 g goat cheese roll

2 sprigs of thyme

1 piece of organic lemon

2 pieces of eggs

150 g sour cream

1 pack of ready-made shortcrust pastry (for quiche and hearty tartes, from Aunt Fanny)

Sea salt and pepper

1. Preheat the oven to 180 degrees. Cut the spring onion into fine rings. Wash and sort blueberries. Cut the goat cheese into cubes.

2. Rinse the thyme sprigs, pluck the leaves off and chop finely. Wash lemon with hot water, rub off. Grate some lemon peel with a very fine grater.

3. Mix the eggs with the sour cream, lemon zest, thyme and goat cheese and season with salt and pepper.

4. Line the springform pan with the shortcrust pastry. Pull up the edge a little and press it into place. Pour in the egg and cheese mixture and spread the blueberries on top.

5. Bake the quiche in the preheated oven for about 40 minutes until it is golden brown. Finally, grind the pepper over it again and let it cool down a little.

Parmigiana with Chicken and Beans

2 servings

Preparation 20 minutes

Preparation time 45 minutes

300 g tomatoes

1 clove of garlic

3 teaspoons of olive oil

1 teaspoon tomato paste

Salt, black pepper

2 sprigs of basil

350 g green beans

0.5 can of white beans (125 g)

250 g chicken breast fillet

0.5 mozzarella

20 g grated parmesan cheese

1. Wash the tomatoes and chop them roughly. Peel the garlic clove, dice it finely and sweat it in 1 teaspoon oil in a small saucepan. Stir in the tomato paste, fry briefly, then add the tomatoes. Simmer in an open pot for 20 minutes, season with salt and pepper, puree. Roughly chop the basil and stir in.

2. Rinse and clean green beans. Cook in boiling salted water for 6–8 minutes so that they are still crisp. Drain and drain. Rinse the white beans in a colander and drain them as well. Rinse the chicken breast, pat dry and cut

into 4–6 pieces. Heat the rest of the olive oil in a non-stick pan and sear the meat on each side so that it is nicely browned. Season with salt and pepper.

3. Spread the chicken breast and both types of beans in a flat baking dish. Pour tomato sauce over it. Finely pluck the mozzarella and sprinkle

with the parmesan. Bake in a preheated oven (200 degrees) for 15–20 minutes.

Zucchini and mozzarella rolls

2 servings

Preparation 20 minutes

Preparation time 45 minutes

1 large straight zucchini

125 g Skyrella (mozzarella from Skyr)

50 g thinly sliced Parma ham (or Serrano ham)

some chili powder

1 spring onion

Salt, black pepper from the mill

1 tbsp olive oil

1 tbsp lemon juice

Toothpicks to stick together

1. Wash the zucchini and rub dry. Then cut lengthways into thin, wide slices with a peeler or a sharp knife. Pluck the Skyrella into small pieces or cut into wafer-thin slices. Pre heat the oven to 180 degrees celcius

2. Cover the most even zucchini slices with mozzarella and ham slices, dust with chili and roll up evenly. Pin in place with a toothpick. Place the rolls

side by side in a small, fire-proof baking dish. Finely chop the rest of the zucchini fringes and spring onions. Add to the rolls in the baking dish.

3. Season with salt and pepper from the mill. Drizzle with olive oil and lemon juice. Bake in the preheated oven for about 20 minutes.

Quick snacks

Tomato Broccoli Soup

2 servings

Preparation 15 minutes

Preparation time 15 minutes

2 small cans of tomatoes

1000 ml of broth

4 tomatoes

200 g broccoli

200 g mushrooms

1 bunch of chives

Salt pepper

1. Drain canned tomatoes (use tomato juice elsewhere) and cut into small pieces. Heat in the broth.

2. Quarter the fresh tomatoes. Divide the broccoli into florets. Clean and quarter the mushrooms.

3. Pour everything into the tomato stock and simmer for about 15 minutes. Cut the chives into rolls and add them. Season to taste with salt and pepper.

Fresh crab salad

4 servings

Preparation 10 minutes

Preparation 5 minutes

3 large radishes

0.5 small red onion

3 stalks of dill

100 g North Sea crab meat

0.5 lemon (juice only)

2 tbsp olive oil

Sea salt, black pepper

1. Wash and clean the radishes and cut into sticks. Peel the onion, dice finely. Chop the dill. Put everything with the crabs in a bowl, stir in the lemon juice and oil. Season well with salt and pepper.

Tip: Goes well with the flea seed Sunday rolls

Spinach salad with asparagus and strawberries

4 servings

Preparation 10 minutes

Preparation 10 minutes

250 g young spinach

250 g green asparagus

3 tbsp olive oil

Sea salt, pepper

75 g pistachios

8 strawberries

1 spring onion

2 tbsp light balsamic vinegar

1. Wash the spinach, sort, cut the stalks if necessary. Divide the leaves between 2 bowls. Wash green asparagus and cut off the ends. Cut the asparagus into slanted 2 cm long pieces. Heat 1 tablespoon of oil in a pan, fry the asparagus for 3-4 minutes and season with salt and pepper. Let cool down briefly and divide into the 2 servings.

2. Remove the pistachios from the shell and roughly chop. Toast in a pan without fat until crispy and golden brown. Spread out on a plate to cool.

3. Wash and clean the strawberries and cut into even slices.

4. Wash and finely chop the spring onions. Mix a dressing from the spring onion, balsamic vinegar and the remaining oil. Season with salt and pepper and drizzle over the salad. Garnish with strawberries and pistachios.

Spicy romaine lettuce with avocado & egg

2 servings

Preparation 10 minutes

Preparation time 30 minutes

2 eggs

1 large romaine lettuce heart

300 g carrots

200 g cherry tomatoes

0.5 cucumber

2 spring onions

1 red pepper

2.5 tbsp lime juice

Salt pepper

2.5 tbsp oil

1 avocado

2 sprigs of fresh oregano

1. Boil the eggs hard for 10 minutes, rinse with cold water and let them cool. Cut the romaine lettuce into wide strips, wash and spin dry.

2. Peel and roughly grate the carrots, wash the cherry tomatoes and cut in half. Wash the cucumber, rub dry, halve lengthways and cut into slices.

3. For the dressing, wash and clean the spring onions and cut into fine rings. Halve the peppers lengthways, remove the stones. Depending on the spiciness (try once), finely dice the whole or only half of the peppers. Mix both with the lime juice, salt and pepper. Withhold the oil.

4. Arrange the lettuce strips in a shallow bowl and spread the carrots,

tomatoes and cucumber on top. Peel and cut the eggs into eighths. Cut the

avocado lengthways around the core. Turn the halves slightly against each other and detach them from each other. Lift out the core with the tip of a spoon.

5. Carefully peel and dice the fruit. Spread the egg and avocado on the salad and drizzle with the dressing. Pluck the oregano leaves from the branches and spread them on the salad - the spicy filling maker is ready!

Dessert

Chocolate brownies

3 servings

Preparation 15 minutes

Preparation in 25 minutes

 1 pinch of cinnamon / 1 pinch of salt

¼ teaspoon baking soda

1 pinch of fresh vanilla

20 g baking cocoa

70 g ground almonds with shell

2 eggs

20 g Xukkolade dark chocolate

20 ml coconut oil

20 g butter

40 g xylitol as a sugar substitute

1. Firstly, preheat the oven to 180 ° C while whipping the whites of 2 eggs with a pinch of salt until stiff. First put the beaten egg white in the cold.

2. Melt the xukkolade, butter and oil in a bowl and then mix all the other ingredients except the egg whites with the liquid. A relatively solid mass should be created.

3. Carefully lift the egg whites under the mass. Now fill everything into a small mold that you laid out with parchment paper beforehand. Baking as a

cake in a cake pan is also possible.

4. Bake the dough for about 20-27 minutes at 180 ° C, depending on the height of the pan, and serve with liquid xukcolade or almond slivers as a decoration.

Homemade strawberry ice cream with skyr

2 servings

Preparation 5 minutes

(Attention, freeze bananas 1 day in advance!)

Preparation 10 minutes

150 g. frozen Strawberries

150 g. frozen banana slices

50 g. Skyr

0.5   limes

Some water

1. Put everything in a multi-chopper

2. Mix all ingredients until a creamy consistency is achieved. Be careful not to add too much water so that the ice does not become too thin, but enough so that it reaches the desired consistency. Just add liquid little by little.

Sugar-free recipes

Fruity chia pudding

2 servings

Prepare overnight

Preparation 10 minutes

200 ml almond milk

1 pinch of fresh vanilla

2 tbsp baking cocoa

40 g chia seeds

100 g raspberries

2 tbsp cocoa nibs

1. Mix the almond milk thoroughly with the vanilla and cocoa powder and then stir the chia seeds into the liquid. Let the mixture swell untouched for about 10 minutes.

2. Stir the mixture again and then divide it into two vessels. Cover the pudding and place in the refrigerator to swell for at least 8 hours.

3. Wash the raspberries or allow frozen products to thaw appropriately. Pick some raspberries for the decoration and puree the rest with a hand blender.

4. Distribute the raspberry puree evenly between the two vessels and garnish the pudding with the raspberries and cocoa nibs.

Our tip: The chia pudding can also be served with other types of fruit and other toppings and is also possible without adding cocoa. Let your imagination run wild and create exciting alternatives to the conventional, sugary breakfast!

Black Forest cake

1 cake

Preparation 30 minutes

Preparation 2.5 hours

3 ½ tbsp coconut oil

3 eggs

80 ml oat drink

1 tbsp date syrup

160 g wholemeal spelled flour

4 tbsp baking cocoa

salt

1 ½ tbsp baking powder

50 g ground almonds

250 g yogurt

125 g quark

4 tbsp rice syrup

1 pinch of fresh vanilla

100 ml milk

1 pack of agar-agar

75 g cream

1 glass of cherries

4 tbsp cocoa nibs

1. Preheat the oven to 175 ° C and grease a 26 cm springform pan. Separate the eggs and beat the egg whites until stiff. Now liquefy the coconut oil by heating it up and mix it with the date syrup and the oat drink as well as the egg yolk.

2. Mix the flour, ground almonds, cocoa, a pinch of salt and baking powder and add the oat drink mixture. Mix everything into a smooth dough and carefully fold in the egg whites.

3. Now divide the dough into three equal parts and bake each dough in the mold for about 8-10 minutes. In the meantime you can prepare the filling: put the quark, yoghurt, rice syrup and vanilla in a bowl.

4. Boil the milk in a small saucepan and stir in the agar agar. Then slowly add the curd mixture. Also, fold in the whipped cream. After draining, the cherries can also be folded in. The same goes for the cocoa nibs. Tip: Put some nibs and cherries aside for decoration if needed.

5. Now layer a bottom with a third of the filling on top of each other. The top layer therefore consists of filling and can be garnished with the leftover cocoa nibs and cherries. Put the mold in the cold for at least two hours and only remove the cake from the mold just before serving. Good Appetite!

Stew with coconut and beans

3 servings

Preparation 20 minutes

Preparation time in 60 minutes

salt and pepper

olive oil

soy sauce

2 stalks of fresh coriander

3 bay leaves

3 tbsp lime juice

1 teaspoon cumin / 1 teaspoon turmeric

1 chili pepper

3-4 spring onions

3-4 carrots

200 g coconut milk

200 g each of white beans, kidney beans and peas

1. Boil the kidney beans and white beans in water for about 40-50 minutes. Meanwhile, you can cut the spring onions and carrots into small slices. Chop the chili well.

2. Heat some olive oil in a wok and add cumin and turmeric. After a few minutes, add the carrots and chili pepper and sauté for about 5 minutes.

3. Pour the coconut milk, 200 ml of water and the bay leaves into the wok and stir everything well. After cooking, add the beans and peas and simmer

over medium heat for about 20 minutes.

4. Meanwhile, finely chop the coriander. After cooking, taste the stew with soy sauce, lime juice, coriander, salt and pepper and let it steep for another 5 minutes. Enjoy your meal

Cauliflower casserole with ham

3-4 servings

Preparation 10 minutes

Preparation time in 60 minutes

1 cauliflower

4 potatoes

200 g cooked ham

150 g of grated cheese

80 g parmesan

2 egg yolks

250 ml of cream

100 ml soy milk

2 cloves of garlic

1 tbsp flour

¼ bunch of chives

½ lime

70 g butter

Nutmeg, salt and pepper

1. Firstly, preheat the oven to 200 ° C. Peel the potatoes and cut them into small cubes. Wash and cut the cauliflower and cook the florets with the potatoes in salted water for at least 5 minutes.

2. Cut the ham into small cubes and grease the baking dish well. Put the vegetables in and spread the ham evenly over them.

3. For the sauce, press the garlic and finely chop the chives. Fry both with 50 g butter and then slowly add soy milk and flour. Add the cream and parmesan and stir everything well. Season to taste with nutmeg, salt and pepper. Take the sauce off the stove and separate the eggs. Now add the egg yolks to the sauce.

4. Pour the sauce evenly over the vegetables and carefully distribute the grated cheese over the casserole. Now bake everything in the oven for 20-30 minutes until golden.

Christmas cookies without sugar

Preparation 1.5 hours

Preparation in 20 minutes

240 g dates

3 teaspoons of gingerbread spices or other Christmas spice mixes

1 teaspoon Baking powder

5 tbsp cocoa powder

100 g coconut oil

100 g ground hazelnuts

100 g ground almonds

300 g spelled flour

1. Pour about 200 ml of very hot water over the dates and let everything stand for about half an hour. During this time you can melt the coconut oil in a saucepan and let it cool down.

2. After soaking, puree the dates in the water and add the dry ingredients and coconut oil. Knead everything well into a dough.

3. Roll out the dough thinly and cut out different cookie shapes. Bake the biscuits on a baking sheet lined with baking paper for 15 - 20 minutes at 170 ° C top and bottom heat. If necessary, you can decorate the Christmas cookies as you like or make them colorful.

Delicious breakfast muffins

6 servings

Preparation 5 minutes

Preparation in 20 minutes

30 g of oatmeal

1 banana

1 tbsp ground almonds

1 teaspoon chia seeds

1 egg

½ teaspoon baking powder

1 teaspoon honey

1 teaspoon peanut butter

40 g raspberries

1. Preheat the oven to 220 ° C. Mash the ripe banana and put the sauce in a bowl. Mix the banana puree and all the other ingredients except the raspberries into a batter.

2. Carefully fold the raspberries into the batter and put everything in a muffin pan. Bake the dough in the preheated oven for about 5 minutes.

3. Turn the oven down to around 180 ° C and bake the muffins for another 12 minutes. It will be a great start to the day!

Refreshing lemonade

1 liter

Preparation 5 minutes

1000 ml of mineral water

Ice cubes

3 tbsp ginger juice

2 lemons

(Some stevia to sweeten if necessary)

1. Put the mineral water in a large container, for example a carafe, and add the ginger juice. Depending on your personal preferences, you can choose sparkling or non-sparkling mineral water.

2. Squeeze the two lemons and add the fresh juice to the lemonade. Add the ice cubes and stir everything briefly. You can then serve the cold refreshment

Oatmeal cup with yogurt & berries

12 servings

Preparation 10 minutes

Preparation time 15 minutes

salt

1 pinch of cinnamon

125 g mixed berries or raspberries

250 g natural yogurt

125 g of crispy oat flakes

100 g honey

2 bananas

1. Mash the bananas with a fork until they become uniform and add the honey. Mix the oatmeal with a pinch of cinnamon and add the mixture to the banana puree.

2. Place 2 tablespoons of each batter in a muffin pan. Press the dough to the edge so that a hollow forms in the middle. Bake the bowls in the oven at 175 ° C for 10-12 minutes.

3. Take the small bowls out of the mold after baking and fill each with about 2 tablespoons of yoghurt. Brush this into the hollow.

4. Decorate each bowl with a few berries. Good Appetite!

Fruity popsicle

2 servings

Preparation 10 minutes

Preparation at least 6 hours

100 g ripe peaches

100 g ripe mango

6 strawberries

250 ml whole milk

1. Peel the mango and peach and remove the stones. Cut the peach and mango into small cubes.

2. Add the milk to the cubes and puree everything to a liquid mass.

3. Cut the strawberries into small slices and fill in ice cream molds. Add the mango milk and put everything in the freezer for at least 6 hours.

4. To loosen the ice from the mold, you can hold it briefly under hot water. Fresh and fruity refreshment on warm summer days!

Bake sugar-free bread yourself

1 bread

Preparation 45 minutes

Preparation time 35 minutes

250 g buckwheat flour

200 g rice flour

100 g mixed grains to taste

1 teaspoon salt

3 teaspoons of bread spice

1 teaspoon stevia

½ pack of sourdough extract

¾ pack of dry yeast

450 ml buttermilk

1. Put the buttermilk, buckwheat flour, rice flour, grains, salt, bread spices, stevia, sourdough extract and dry yeast in a bowl in the order listed and knead everything thoroughly with a dough hook.

2. Shape the dough into a loaf and place it on a baking sheet lined with parchment paper or greased. Let the loaf rise for 35 minutes.

3. Then bake the bread for 35 minutes at 205 ° C. Slice it warm and enjoy!

Homemade tomato ketchup

500 milliliters of ketchup

Preparation 10 minutes

Preparation in 20 minutes

1 clove of garlic

2 shallots

1 tbsp olive oil

2 teaspoons of curry

1 teaspoon pepper

1 pinch of salt

Ginger powder

chili

1 tbsp cornstarch

500 ml of pureed tomatoes

1. Chop the onions and squeeze the garlic. Put both in a saucepan and sweat it with a little olive oil. Then add the tomatoes and let everything simmer for about 20 minutes. While doing this, stir occasionally.

2. Take everything off the stove and let it cool down briefly. Then add the spices and puree everything with the hand blender to a fine mass.

3. Pour the ketchup into sterile containers while it is still hot, for example into boiled mason jars. Cap the jars immediately to ensure shelf life. The

ketchup can be kept for about a month when sealed and about a week after opening.

Our tip: The homemade ketchup is a great souvenir at parties and a personal gift for hosts.

Couscous with tofu and spinach

4 servings

Preparation in 20 minutes

pepper and salt

½ teaspoon ground coriander

½ teaspoon cumin

100 ml coconut milk

3 tbsp olive oil

100 smoked tofu

50 g cashew nuts

1 red onion

1 clove of garlic

500 spinach

150 couscous

1. Boil 300 ml of water and add a little salt. Pour it over the couscous and let it swell.

2. Wash the spinach thoroughly and drain it. Chop much of the spinach and set the rest aside.

3. Peel and chop the onion and garlic. Also, chop the cashew nuts into small pieces. Crumble the tofu and put everything together in a pan and fry it with a little fat.

4. Add the chopped spinach and wait for it to collapse slightly.

5. Stir in the couscous and add the coconut milk. Season everything well with coriander, salt, pepper and caraway seeds.

6. Finally fold in the unchopped spinach leaves. Just serve - done!

Pizza with cauliflower batter

4 small or 2 large servings

Preparation 20 minutes

Preparation in 20 minutes

1 bunch of rocket

4 slices of Parma ham

100 ml tomato sauce

2 teaspoons of oregano

75 g mini mozzarella

50 g mushrooms

salt

2 tbsp grated cheese

1 tbsp ground almonds

1 egg

500 g fresh cauliflower

1. Preheat the oven to 200 ° C fan oven. First of all, you need to wash and clean the cauliflower and finely grate it with a grater. Bake the cauliflower powder on a baking sheet lined with baking paper for about 10 minutes.

2. Put the powder on a tea towel and use it to squeeze out the water. This may take a while, but a surprising amount of water will leak out.

3. Mix the dry cauliflower with the egg, almonds and grated cheese in a bowl. Season the dough with salt and shape it on a tray into 4 small or 2 large pizzas.

4. Pre-bake the dough at 200 ° C for about 10 minutes. Meanwhile, you can clean the mushrooms and cut them into pieces. Dice the mozzarella and coat the pizzas with the tomato sauce. Top with mozzarella, mushrooms, and oregano.

5. Bake the pizzas for another 10 minutes and then add the Parma ham and rocket. The pizzas are served hot immediately!

Tuna Egg Muffins

4 servings

Preparation 10 minutes

Preparation time 15 minutes

5 eggs

1 can of tuna

10 black pitted olives

1 hand of parsley

100 grams of cherry tomatoes

100 grams of paprika

30 ml. Milk

1 small onion

Salt / pepper / paprika powder

1. Preheat the oven to 200 ° C fan oven. Grease the muffin pan or use silicone molds.

2. Put the eggs in a bowl and whisk with the milk.

3. Cut the olives, peppers, onions and tomatoes into small cubes or quarters. Then roughly chop the parsley.

4. Drain the tuna and fold into the egg mixture with the tomatoes, onions, olives, bell pepper and parsley.

5. Season with salt, pepper and the paprika powder

6. Bake at 200 ° C for approx. 12 minutes until the muffins are golden yellow.

Tip: Great as a meal prep

Sugar-free banana pancakes

2 servings

Preparation 10 minutes

Preparation time 45 minutes

125 g wheat flour

1 teaspoon Baking powder

125 ml milk

1 medium-sized egg

salt

1 teaspoon oil

1 medium banana

2 tbsp rice syrup

1. Mix the flour, salt, baking powder and milk into a dough and let rise for half an hour.

2. Then add the egg and stir again.

3. Heat a dash of oil in the pan and bake two pancakes from the batter. Cover with the slices of half a banana and turn once in the pan. Brush with rice syrup and serve.

hazelnut cake

20 servings

Preparation 15 minutes

Preparation time 35 minutes

600 g hazelnuts (ground)

9 medium-sized eggs

300 g xylitol

1 teaspoon cloves (ground)

1.5 teaspoons of cinnamon

0.5 tsp cardamom (ground)

0.5 tsp nutmeg

0.5 tsp anise

1 pack of baking powder

1. Preheat the oven to 170 degrees (convection).

2. Mix the ingredients in the bowl with the mixer to form dough.

3. Grease the baking pan with butter, pour in the batter.

4. Bake for about 35 minutes.

Refreshing cherry and yogurt ice cream

3-4 servings

Preparation 10 minutes

Preparation 10 minutes

200 g frozen cherries, unsweetened

200 g frozen banana slices

100 g low-fat yogurt

Juice of half a lemon

Vanilla pulp from half a pod

1. Mix the cherries, banana slices and yoghurt for about 5 minutes in the multimixer until the consistency is creamy. (Every now and then, smooth down a little with a rubber spatula.)

2. Add the lemon juice and the vanilla pulp and mix again for 1 minute.

3. Serve in a glass.

Tip: Cherries can be replaced by all kinds of unsweetened frozen fruit!

Sugar-free lemon and orange iced tea

4 servings

Preparation 10 minutes

Preparation time in 60 minutes

1000 ml of water

3 bags of green tea

16 ice cubes

1 medium orange (organic)

1 medium lemon (organic)

1/2 medium lime

Some fresh mint

1. Prepare the tea according to the instructions. Then remove the tea bags and let the tea cool down.

2. Then put the tea with half of the ice cubes in a jug and chill in the refrigerator for about an hour.

3. In the meantime, cut the orange and lemon into thin slices. Squeeze the lime.

4. After the tea has become refreshingly cold in the refrigerator, add the orange and lemon and refine with the juice of the lime and mint. Sweeten with a little honey if necessary. Serve the iced tea with 2 ice cubes per glass.

Sugar-free & healthy brownies

1 serving

Preparation 15 minutes

Preparation in 40 minutes

1 can of black beans (drained weight 250 g)

2 eggs

5 pitted dates

50 g cocoa powder without sugar

80 ml maple syrup or agave syrup

1 TEASPOON. Vanilla extract

0.5 tsp. Baking soda

1 pinch of salt

120 g butter

80 g pecans

1. Preheat the oven to 170 ° C circulating air (190 ° C top and bottom heat) and line or grease a rectangular baking pan measuring approx. 21 x 24 cm with baking paper.

2. Melt the butter and let it cool down a bit. Grind the drained beans, eggs, dates, cocoa powder, maple syrup, vanilla extract, baking soda and salt in the food processor and then puree until smooth. Then pour in the melted butter while the machine is running

3. Pour the dough into the prepared mold and smooth the surface by gently tapping the mold. Roughly chop the pecans and spread them on the surface of the brownies.

4. Bake the brownies on the middle rack for about 40 minutes, until the baked goods are firm and the surface is slightly cracked. Remove the brownies and let them cool completely.

If the surface of the brownies browns too quickly, cover the baking pan with aluminum foil halfway through the baking time.

Sugar-free apple pie

4 servings

Preparation 20 minutes

Preparation time 50 minutes

For the dough:

500 g margarine

480 g erythritol (sugar substitute)

1200 g of flour

8 egg yolks

4 egg whites

4 teaspoons of baking powder

For the filling:

4 kg of apple

some erythritol (sugar substitute)

some cinnamon

some vanilla

some lemon juice

For covering:

300 g erythritol (sugar substitute)

300 g butter

300 g almonds, chopped or sliced

8 egg whites

1. Peel and dice the apples for the filling and sauté with a little erythritol (I use No Sugar Sugar), lemon juice, cinnamon and vanilla in the pan until the apples are soft. Mix the egg yolks and whites with the sugar substitute and margarine until frothy. Gradually stir in the flour and baking powder to make a shortcrust pastry. Divide the dough and press part of it into a greased springform pan, pulling up the edge a little. Spread the steamed apples on the dough. Roll out the second part of the shortcrust pastry and place on top of the filling.

2. Then beat 2 egg whites until stiff, stir in the remaining ingredients for the topping and fold in the egg whites. Spread the topping on the cake in the springform pan.

3. Bake the cake for approx. 40 minutes at 175 ° C. After 20 minutes prick the pastry cover several times with a fork so that the moisture can escape.

Crispy chicken legs with red cabbage salad

4 servings

Preparation 35 minutes

Preparation time 45 minutes

300 g Greek yogurt

2 teaspoons of mustard

2 teaspoons maple syrup

1 tsp Tabasco

salt

pepper

8 medium-sized chicken legs

100 g corn flakes

100 g potato chips (baked)

1/4 clove garlic (powder)

1/2 teaspoon paprika powder

250 g red cabbage (fresh!)

250 g sugar snap peas

3 tbsp apple cider vinegar

1. Whisk the yoghurt, mustard, maple syrup, Tabasco and ½ teaspoon each of salt and pepper in a bowl. Half of it goes in the refrigerator. Marinate the chicken drumsticks with the rest and put them in a roaster for about 30 minutes.

2. Crush cornflakes and potato chips with a mortar or grind them in a plastic bag with a rolling pin. Add the garlic and paprika powder as well as ½ teaspoon each of salt and pepper, distribute everything together on a flat plate.

3. Preheat the oven to 200 degrees. Take the marinated chicken legs out of the refrigerator and turn them in the breading. Place the chicken legs on a parchment-lined baking sheet. Bake for about 35 minutes, until the meat is golden brown and crispy.

4. Meanwhile, cut the red cabbage and the sugar snap peas into fine pieces. Mix the remaining marinade from the refrigerator with apple cider vinegar and mix everything together. To serve, arrange 2 chicken legs with coleslaw on a plate.

Asian duck salad

2 servings

Preparation 25 minutes

Preparation in 25 minutes

200 g duck breast

20 g Lucerne sprouts

2 handfuls of coriander (fresh)

150 g red cabbage (raw, cut into strips)

150 g white cabbage (raw, cut into strips)

160 g carrots

2 tbsp sesame seeds (toasted)

For the dressing:

4 tbsp soy sauce

2 tbsp rice wine vinegar

1 teaspoon brown sugar

2 tbsp olive oil

1 pod of chili (red)

1. Fry the duck breast until pink and cut into fine strips.

2. Slice or cut the cabbage into strips and chop the carrots into fine strips.

3. Wash the sprouts and coriander, finely chop the coriander. Mix the vegetables together, place the duck breast on top and sprinkle with the sesame seeds.

4. For the dressing, finely chop the chili pepper and mix it with the soy sauce, rice wine vinegar, olive oil and sugar and pour over the salad.

Potato salad with apple and egg

4 servings

Preparation 40 minutes

Preparation in 25 minutes

300 g potatoes (cooked)

2 medium-sized tomatoes

2 medium-sized pickles

1 medium apple

1 medium onion

1/2 medium bell pepper

For the dressing:

1 medium-sized egg (hard-boiled)

1/2 tbsp mustard (medium hot)

3 tbsp olive oil

1 tbsp white wine vinegar

1/2 teaspoon xucker

1 pinch of salt

1 pinch of pepper

1. Peel off the boiled potatoes, peel the tomatoes and then dice them. Also, cut the cucumber, apple, bell pepper and onion into small pieces and mix together.

2. Dressing: cut the egg in half, remove the yolk, mash with a fork and stir with mustard. Finely dice the egg white, then add to the other ingredients.

3. Add oil, vinegar, salt, pepper, xucker. Season to taste. Add to the salad, mix well. Let it steep for 30 minutes.

4. Garnish with egg eighths, tomato slices, parsley and paprika powder.

Salad with potatoes tuna and egg

2 servings

Preparation 15 minutes

Preparation time 15 minutes

2 cans of tuna in its own juice

4 medium potatoes (cooked, sliced)

2 medium-sized tomatoes

2 medium-sized eggs (hard-boiled, sliced)

150 g green beans (steamed)

2 tbsp olive oil

2 tbsp balsamic vinegar

1. Drain the tuna, cut the tomatoes into large pieces and place in a large bowl with the potato slices and beans.

2. Mix the vinegar and oil well, pour over the salad, mix.

3. Finally, put the egg slices on top.

Sugar-free walnut raspberry muffins

10 servings

Preparation 15 minutes

Preparation time 35 minutes

100 g raspberries

4 medium-sized eggs

1 pinch of salt

1/2 teaspoon baking powder

2 tbsp xylitol

200 g almonds (ground)

90 ml rapeseed oil

15 g walnuts

1 teaspoon chia seeds

1. If necessary, let the raspberries thaw beforehand if frozen berries are used

2. Meanwhile, separate the eggs and beat the egg white with a pinch of salt until stiff.

3. Mix the egg yolks with the baking powder and the oil in another bowl, mix in the chia seeds, xylitol, ground almonds and walnuts. Then carefully fold in the stiffly beaten egg white. Finally, add the raspberries.

4. Pour the mixture into muffin molds and bake in the oven at 175 ° C for about 20-25 minutes.

Smoothies

Breakfast smoothie # 1
1 large, ripe banana
4 dates
2 tablespoons of oatmeal
2 tsp chia seeds
300ml milk

Breakfast smoothie # 2
1 banana
1 handful of fresh or frozen spinach
1 orange
1 ripe, soft avocado
200ml water

Detox smoothie
2 tablespoons of lemon juice
1 slice of ginger
1 sweet apple
1 ripe pear
1 beetroot
1 carrot

Vitamin smoothie
1 orange
½ lime

2 small carrots

1 slice of ginger

a tablespoon of linseed oil

200ml water

Per-work-out smoothie

1 handful of strawberries

½ lime

1 banana

100g yogurt of your choice

200ml milk

After-work-out smoothie

1 banana

3 dried dates or 2 tbsp raisins

1 tablespoon of oatmeal

1 teaspoon of peanut butter

1 teaspoon pumpkin seeds

150ml milk of your choice

Cherry smoothie

1 tablespoon of peanut butter

150g cherries

1 small banana

150ml milk

Healthy life smoothie

400ml water

300g romaine lettuce

½ bunch of baby spinach

3 celery

1 apple

1 pear

1 banana

½ lemon

Fruit smoothie

½ apple

½ orange

1 passion fruit

Fresh mint

¼ honeydew melon

1 slice of ginger

1 pinch of salt

Kefir smoothie

400ml kefir

5 tablespoons of whole sea buckthorn fruit

2 tablespoons of agave syrup

2 tablespoons of wheat bran

½ handful of crash ice

Avocado smoothie # 2

1 bunch of coriander

2 avocados

500ml kefir

1 lime
1 teaspoon wasabi pie
500g Skyr
Salt pepper

Grapefruit and spinach smoothie

150g baby spinach
1 ½ grapefruit
1 stalk of celery
Juice of half a lemon
150ml water

Algae and kale smoothie

1 handful of kale
2 handfuls of lamb's lettuce
½ avocado
1 pear
1 teaspoon coconut oil
1 teaspoon of chlorella
300ml coconut water

Banana and raspberry smoothie

1 banana
150g raspberries
150g baby spinach
2 teaspoons of soaked chia seeds
150ml water

Beetroot and ginger smoothie

1 beetroot

1 apple

1 carrot

1 small pak choi

1 slice of ginger

1 orange

Banana and peach smoothie

2 bananas

3 peaches

1 orange

500ml coconut milk

4 ice cubes

Superfood smoothie

1 pineapple

1 handful of watercress

1 handful of kale

300ml coconut milk

2 tablespoons of chia seeds

Healthy smoothie

100g broccoli (cooked)

1 apple

2 kiwis

2 handfuls of baby spinach

200ml naturally cloudy apple juice

200ml water

Power drink smoothie

1 sprig of basil

1 kiwi

1 mango

1 bunch of watercress

1 apple

1 quince

1 tablespoon of oxalis

2 tablespoons of lime juice

3 tablespoons of agave syrup

Chocolate banana smoothie

2 ripe bananas

1 teaspoon cocoa

500ml milk

Mango and spinach smoothie

1 handful of baby spinach

1 tablespoon of lemon juice

1 banana

½ mango

250ml water

Pinkie smoothie

150g raspberries

300ml milk

1 banana

The berry smoothie

120g fresh strawberries

60g blueberries

300ml milk

1 tablespoon of agave syrup

Blood orange smoothie

1/2 beetroot

1 blood orange

1 carrot

1 lemon

1 slice of ginger

cinnamon

200ml water

Matcha green smoothie

¼ pineapple

¼ avocado

1 lemon with 250ml water

3 dates

Handful of spinach

Handful of cashew nuts

½ teaspoon matcha

Turmeric and Coconut Smoothie

1 banana

1 lemon

1 tablespoon of chia seeds

1 pinch of pepper

1 tablespoon of turmeric

200ml coconut milk

100ml water

Green tea mango smoothie

Green tea

1 ripe mango

2 tablespoons

Organic whole grain oat flakes

1-2 tablespoons of organic agave syrup

Pick-me-up smoothie

2 kiwi

1 teaspoon of linseed oil

2 boiled carrots

200ml water

some mint

Golden yogurt smoothie

1 slice of ginger

150g yogurt

2 tablespoons of agave syrup

100ml almond milk

1 pinch of black ground pepper

1 pinch of cardamom ground

1 pinch of ground cinnamon

1 teaspoon ground turmeric

Beauty smoothie

2 oranges

1 pink grapefruit

500ml buttermilk

30g tender oat flakes

2 tablespoons of honey

Pear and mango smoothie

100g fresh spinach

1 ripe pear

1 banana

½ mango

100ml water

Lime and buttermilk smoothie

2 tablespoons of agave syrup

½ teaspoon lime zest

1 tablespoon of lime juice

500ml buttermilk

100g raspberries

Indian mango smoothie

2 mango

150ml orange juice

250g yogurt

1 tablespoon of brown sugar

2 teaspoons of lemon juice

1 teaspoon coconut syrup

Coconut and raspberry smoothie
300g raspberries
200g baby spinach
250ml coconut water
½ cucumber
½ avocado

Tropical green smoothie
½ head of romaine lettuce
½ pineapple
1 mango
1 slice of ginger
100ml water

Vital smoothie
1 avocado
1 cucumber
200g spinach
2 large leaves of kale
2 leaves of cabbage
Juice of 3 lemons
1 green apple
250ml coconut water

Kiwi and avocado smoothie
2 kiwis

1 banana

1 mango

10 kale leaves

1 avocado

200ml water

Pear and banana smoothie

2 bananas

2 pears

6 cabbage leaves

250ml coconut water

Super wheatgrass smoothie

2 bananas

½ avocado

2 cups of fresh wheatgrass

½ romaine lettuce heart

1 mango

300ml water

Banana Boost Smoothie

1 banana

150g baby spinach

1 tablespoon of flaxseed

2 tablespoons of protein powder

1 tablespoon of maca powder

200ml coconut water

Pineapple and cherry smoothie

½ pineapple

150g cherries (pitted)

200ml cherry juice

100ml coconut water

Mango smoothie

1 mango

3 oranges

Juice of 1 lime

1 pinch of turmeric

Citrus fruit smoothie

2 blood oranges

Juice of 1 lime

½ pomelo

200ml coconut water

Melon and strawberry smoothie

½ net melon

1 orange

200g strawberries

100ml water

Coconut and passion fruit smoothie

1 banana

350ml passion fruit juice

200ml coconut water

100g yogurt

¼ vanilla stick (vanilla pulp)

Orange and peanut smoothie

4 oranges

150g grapes

1 tablespoon unsalted peanuts

3 teaspoons of honey

50ml oat milk

Celery, spinach and apple smoothie

1 apple

1 banana

1 orange

1 stick of celery

1 handful of spinach

Some arugula

¼ cucumber

200ml. water

Orange and strawberry smoothie

200g strawberries

Juice of 3 oranges

1 banana

2 mint leaves

Mango and pineapple smoothie

½ mango

¼ pineapple

1 banana

orange juice

100ml coconut milk

Almond yogurt smoothie

1 apple

1 banana

5 raw almonds

175g low-fat Greek yogurt

100ml low-fat milk

a pinch of cinnamon

CPSIA information can be obtained
at www.ICGtesting.com
Printed in the USA
LVHW011732050721
691861LV00006B/210

9 789018 215422